P9-DHB-938

and thinking

NOW

WHAT

ACKNOWLEDGMENTS:

I would like to thank everybody

at the University of the Arts in Philadelphia for asking me to come and talk to them and making me so welcome when I did — in particular, my thanks go to Carise Mitch, to Dean Christopher Sharrock (the nattiest man there), and to President Sean T. Buffington.

AMANDA PALMER LISTENED TO THIS SPEECH THREE

times, each time I rewrote it, and she did not let me get away with anything. Her speech to the New England Institute of Arts in 2011, on the **Fraud Police** showed me that you could tell people real things, and not have them pelt you with fruit and

beer cans.

I
love
her,

and am grateful to her.

This speech was originally delivered to the University of the Arts Class of 2012, and you can watch me saying it at http://vimeo.com/42372767

Gaiman

THE

MAKE GOOD ART

SPEECH

Also by Neil Gaiman

WILLIAM MORROW An Imprint of HarperCollinsPublishers

MAKE GOOD ART. Copyright ©
2013 by Neil Gaiman. Images for
MAKE GOOD ART copyright
© 2013 by Chip Kidd. All rights
reserved. Printed in China.
No part of this book may be used
or reproduced in any manner
whatsoever without written
permission except in the case
of brief quotations embodied in
critical articles and reviews. For
information address Harper-
Collins Publishers, 10 East 53rd
Street, New York, NY 10022.

HarperCollins books may be
purchased for educational,
business, or sales promotional
use. For information please
write: Special Markets
Department, HarperCollins
Publishers, 10 East 53rd Street,
New York, NY 10022.

FIRST EDITION

Designed by Chip Kidd

Library of Congress Cataloging-in-Publication Data has been applied for.

ISBN 978-0-06-2266767-

19 14 15 16 17   ov RRD   10 9 8 7 6 5 4 3 2 1

17 May 2012

"I never really expected to find myself giving advice to people graduating from an establishment of higher education. I never graduated from any such establishment. I never even started at one. I **escaped** from school

as soon as I could, when the prospect of

four

more

years

of

enforced learning before I'd become the writer I wanted to be
was stifling.

I got out into the world, I wrote, and I became a better writer the more I wrote, and I wrote some more, and nobody ever seemed to mind that I was making it up as I went along, they just read what I wrote and they paid for it, **or they didn't**, and often they commissioned me to write something else for them.

Which has left me with a healthy respect

and fondness for higher education

that those of my friends and family,

were cured of long ago.

Looking back,
I've had a remarkable ride.
I'm not sure I can call it a **CAREER**,
because a **CAREER** implies that I had
some kind of **CAREER** plan, and I

never did. The nearest thing I had was a list I made when I was 15 of everything I wanted to do:

to write an adult novel,

a children's book,

a comic,

a movie,

record an audiobook,

write an episode of *Doctor Who*

. . . and so on.

I DIDN'T HAVE A CAREER.

I just did the next thing on the list.

So I thought I'd tell you

everything I wish I'd known

starting out, and a few things that,

looking back on it, I suppose that I did

know. And that I would also give you

the best piece of advice I'd ever got,

which I completely

failed to

follow.

1irst of all:

When you start out on a career in the arts you have no idea what you are doing.

THIS
IS GREAT.
PEOPLE WHO

know what they are doing

know the rules,

and know what is

possible and

impossible.

You do not.

The rules on what is possible and impossible in

the arts were made by people who had not tested

the bounds of the possible by going beyond them.

If you don't know
it's impossible
it's easier
to do.

AND BECAUSE NOBODY'S DONE IT BEFORE,
THEY HAVEN'T MADE UP RULES TO STOP ANYONE
DOING THAT AGAIN,
YET.

2ECONDLY:

If you have an idea of what you want to make,

what you were put here to do,

then just go and do that.

And that's much harder than it sounds and, sometimes in the end, *so much easier than you might imagine.*

Because normally, there are things you have to do before you can get to the place you want to be. I wanted to write comics and novels and stories and films, so I became a journalist, because journalists are allowed to ask questions, and to simply go and find out how the world works, and besides, to do those things I needed to write and to write well, and I was being paid to learn how to write economically, crisply, sometimes under adverse conditions, and on time.

Sometimes the way to do what you hope to do will be clear cut, and sometimes it will be almost impossible to decide whether or not you are doing the correct thing, because you'll have to balance your goals and hopes with feeding yourself, paying debts, finding work, settling for what you can get.

Something that worked for me
was imagining that where I wanted to be

{ an author, primarily of fiction, making good books, making good comics, and supporting myself through my words }

was a mountain.

A d i s t a n t m o u n t a i n.

M y g o a l.

And I knew that as long as I kept walking towards the mountain, I would be all right.

And when I truly was not sure what to do, I could stop, and think about whether it was taking me towards or away from the mountain. I said no to editorial jobs on magazines, proper jobs that would have paid proper money, because I knew that, attractive though they were, for me they would have been walking away from the mountain. And if those job offers had come along earlier I might have taken them, because they still would have been closer to the mountain than I was at the time.

I learned to write by writing.

I tended to do anything as long as it felt like an adventure, and to stop when it felt like work, which meant that

life did not feel like work.

3hirdly:

When you start off, you have to deal with the problems of failure. You need to be thick-

skinned, to learn that not every project will survive. A freelance life, a life in the arts, is

sometimes like putting messages in bottles, on a desert island, and hoping that someone will

find one of your bottles and open it and read it, and put something in a bottle that will wash its

way back to you: appreciation, or a commis- sion, or money, or love. And you have to accept

that you may put out a hundred things for every bottle that winds up coming back.

THE PROBLEMS OF FAILURE ARE PROBLEMS OF DISCOURAGEMENT, OF HOPELESSNESS, OF HUNGER. YOU WANT EVERYTHING TO HAPPEN AND YOU WANT IT NOW, AND THINGS GO WRONG.

My first book—a piece of journalism I had done for the money, and which had already bought me an electric typewriter from the advance—should have been a best-seller. It should have paid me a lot of money. If the publisher hadn't gone into involuntary liquidation between the first print run selling out and the second printing, and before any royalties could be paid, it would have done.

And I shrugged,

and I still had my electric typewriter and enough money to pay the rent for a couple of months, and I decided that I would do my best in future not to write books just for the money. If you didn't get the money, then you didn't have anything. If I did work I was proud of, and I didn't get the money, at least I'd have the work.

Every now and again, I forget that rule, and whenever I do, the universe kicks me hard and reminds me. I don't know that it's an issue for anybody but me, but it's true that **nothing I did where the only reason for doing it was the money was ever worth it** except as bitter experience. Usually I didn't wind up getting the money, either. The things I did because I was excited, and wanted to see them exist in reality, have never let me down, and I've never regretted the time I spent on any of them.

THE PROBLEMS OF FAILURE ARE HARD.

The first problem of any kind of even limited success is the unshakable conviction that you are GETTING AWAY WITH SOMETHING, and that any moment now THEY WILL DISCOVER YOU. It's Imposter Syndrome, something my wife Amanda christened THE FRAUD POLICE.

In my case, I was convinced that there would be a knock on the door, and a man with a clipboard **(I DON'T KNOW WHY HE CARRIED A CLIPBOARD, IN MY HEAD, BUT HE DID)** would be there, to tell me **it was all over**, and they had caught up with me, and now I would have to go and get a real job, one that didn't consist of making things up and writing them down, and reading books I wanted to read. And then I would go away quietly and get the kind of job where you don't have to make things up anymore.

The problems of success.
They're real, and with luck you'll experience them.
The point where you

STOP SAYING YES

to everything, because now the bottles you threw
in the ocean are all coming back, and have to

LEARN TO SAY NO.

I watched my peers, and my friends, and the ones who were older than me and watched how miserable some of them were: I'd listen to them telling me that they couldn't envisage a world where they did what they had always wanted to do anymore, because now they had to earn a certain amount every month just to keep where they were. They couldn't go and do the things that mattered, and that they had really wanted to do; and that seemed as big a tragedy as any problem of failure.

And after that, the biggest problem of success is that the world conspires to stop you doing the thing that you do, because you are successful. There was a day when I looked up and realised that I had become someone who professionally replied to email, and who wrote as a hobby. I started answering fewer emails, and was relieved to find I was writing much more.

4ourthly:

I
HOPE
YOU'LL
MAKE
MISTAKES.

IF YOU'RE MAKING MISTAKES, it means you're out there doing something. And the mistakes in themselves can be useful. I once misspelled "Caroline" in a letter, transposing the A and the O, and I thought, "Coraline looks like a real name . . ."

And remember that

whatever discipline you are in,

whether you are a musician

or a photographer,

a fine artist

or a cartoonist, a writer,

a dancer, a designer, whatever

you do, you have one thing that's unique.

You have the ability to make art.

And for me, and for so many of

the people I have known,

that's been a lifesaver.

The ultimate lifesaver.

It gets you through good times

and it gets you through the other ones.

Life is sometimes hard.

Things go wrong, in life and in love

and in business and in friendship and

in health and in all the other ways

that life can go wrong.

And when things get tough,

this is what you should do.

MAKE GOOD ART.
I'M SERIOUS.

HUSBAND RUNS OFF WITH A POLITICIAN?

LEG CRUSHED AND THEN EATEN
BY MUTATED BOA CONSTRICTOR?

IRS ON YOUR TRAIL?

CAT EXPLODED?

SOMEBODY ON THE INTERNET THINKS
WHAT YOU DO IS STUPID OR EVIL OR
IT'S ALL BEEN DONE BEFORE?

PROBABLY THINGS WILL WORK OUT SOME-
HOW, AND EVENTUALLY TIME WILL
TAKE THE STING AWAY,
BUT THAT DOESN'T MATTER.
DO WHAT ONLY YOU DO BEST.

Make
it on the
good days
too.

and 5ifthly,

while you are at it, make *your* art.
Do the stuff that only you can do.

The urge, starting out, is to copy. And that's not a bad thing.
Most of us only find our own voices after we've sounded like a
lot of other people. But the one thing that you have that nobody
else has is *you*. Your voice, your mind, your story, your vision.

SO WRITE AND DRAW AND BUILD AND PLAY
AND DANCE AND LIVE AS ONLY YOU CAN.

The moment that you feel that, just possibly, **YOU'RE WALKING DOWN THE STREET NAKED,** exposing too much of your heart and your mind and what exists on the inside, showing too much of yourself. That's the moment you may be starting to get it right.

The things I've done that worked the best were the things I was the **least** certain about, the stories where I was sure they would either work, or more likely be the kinds of **embarrassing failures** people would gather together and talk about until the end of time. They always had that in common: looking back at them, people explain why they were inevitable successes. While I was doing them,

I HAD NO IDEA.

I STILL DON'T.

And where would be the fun in making something you knew was going to work?

AND SOMETIMES THE THINGS
I DID REALLY DIDN'T WORK.

There are stories of mine that have never been reprinted. Some of them never even left the house.

But I learned as much from them as I did from the things that worked.

6ixthly:

I WILL PASS ON SOME SECRET FREE-
LANCER KNOWLEDGE. **SECRET KNOWL-
EDGE IS ALWAYS GOOD.** AND IT IS USE-
FUL FOR ANYONE WHO EVER PLANS TO
CREATE ART FOR OTHER PEOPLE, TO EN-
TER A FREELANCE WORLD OF ANY KIND. I
LEARNED IT IN COMICS, BUT IT APPLIES
TO OTHER FIELDS TOO. AND IT'S THIS:

People get hired because, somehow, they get hired. In my case
I did something which these days would be easy to check, and
would get me into trouble, and when I started out, in those pre-
Internet days, seemed like a sensible career strategy: when I was
asked by editors who I'd worked for, I lied. I listed a handful of
magazines that sounded likely, and I sounded confident, and I got
jobs. I then made it a point of honour to have written something
for each of the magazines I'd listed to get that first job, so that I
hadn't actually lied, I'd just been chronologically challenged . . .

You get work however you get work.

People keep working, in a freelance world,

and more and more of today's world is freelance,

because

1 their work is good,

2 and because they are easy to get along with,

3 and because they deliver the work on time.

And you don't even need all three.

TWO OUT OF THREE IS FINE.

People
will
tolerate
how
unpleasant
you
are
if
your
work
is
good
and
you
deliver
it
on
time.

They'll forgive the

lateness of the work if it's good,

and if they like you.

And you don't have to be as good as the others if you're on time and it's always a pleasure to hear from you.

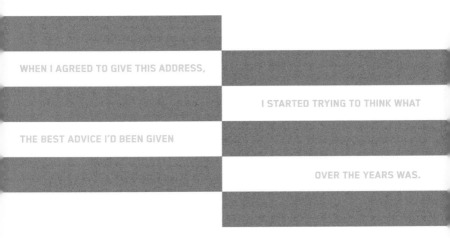

WHEN I AGREED TO GIVE THIS ADDRESS,

I STARTED TRYING TO THINK WHAT

THE BEST ADVICE I'D BEEN GIVEN

OVER THE YEARS WAS.

And it came from

Stephen King

twenty years ago, at the height of the success of

Sandman.

I was writing a comic that people loved and were taking seriously. King had liked *Sandman* and my novel with Terry Pratchett, *Good Omens*, and he saw the madness, the long signing lines, all that, and his advice was this:

And I didn't.

Best advice I got that I ignored.
Instead I worried about it.
I worried about the next deadline,
the next idea, the next story.
There wasn't a moment
for the next fourteen
or fifteen years that
I wasn't writing something
in my head,
or wondering about it.

And I didn't stop and look around and go,
this is really fun.
I wish I'd enjoyed it more.
It's been an amazing ride.
But there were parts of the ride I missed,
because **I was too worried** about things going wrong,
about what came next,
to enjoy the bit I was on.

**THAT WAS THE HARDEST LESSON FOR ME,
I THINK:**

to let go

and enjoy the ride,
because the ride takes you
to some remarkable and unexpected places.

AND HERE,
ON THIS PLATFORM,
TODAY, IS ONE OF THOSE PLACES.
(I AM ENJOYING MYSELF IMMENSELY.)

To all today's graduates:

I wish you luck.
Luck is useful.

Often you will discover that the harder you work,
and the more wisely you work,
the luckier you get.
But there is luck, and it helps.

We're in a transitional world right now, if you're in any kind of artistic field, because the nature of distribution is changing, the models by which creators got their work out into the world, and got to keep a roof over their heads and buy sandwiches while they did that, are all changing. I've talked to people at the top of the food chain in publishing, in bookselling, in all those areas, and nobody knows what the landscape will look like two years from now, let alone a decade away. The distribution channels that people had built over the last century or so are in flux for print, for visual artists, for musicians, for creative people of all kinds.

Which is, on the one hand, **INTIMIDATING**, and on the other, immensely

liberating.

The rules, the assumptions, **the now we're supposed to's** of how you get your work seen, and what you do then, **are breaking down.** The gatekeepers are leaving their gates.

You can be as creative as you need to be to get your work seen.

YouTube and the web (and whatever comes after YouTube and the web) can give you more people watching than television ever did. The old rules are crumbling and nobody knows what the new rules are.

rules.

own

your

up

make

So

Someone asked me recently how to do something she thought was going to be difficult, in this case recording an audiobook, and I suggested she pretend that she was someone who could do it. **Not pretend to do it, but pretend she was someone who could.** She put up a notice to this effect on the studio wall, and she said it helped.

So be wise, because the world needs more wisdom.

AND IF YOU CANNOT BE WISE, PRETEND TO BE SOMEONE WHO IS WISE, AND THEN JUST BEHAVE LIKE THEY WOULD.

And now **go,** and

MAKE INTERESTING AMAZING GLORIOUS FANTASTIC MISTAKES.

Break.

Leave the world more interesting for your being here.

Make

good

art.

clap clap clap clap clap clap clap clap clap clap clap clap clap clap clap clap clap clap clap clap
clap clap clap clap clap clap clap clap clap clap clap clap clap clap clap clap clap clap clap clap cla
clap clap clap clap clap clap clap clap clap clap clap clap clap clap clap clap clap clap clap clap cl
clap clap clap clap clap clap clap clap clap clap clap clap clap clap clap clap clap clap clap clap clap
clap clap clap clap clap clap clap clap clap clap clap clap clap clap woo-hoo!! clap clap clap
clap clap clap clap clap clap clap clap clap clap clap clap clap clap clap clap clap clap clap clap clap
clap clap clap clap clap clap clap clap clap clap clap clap clap clap clap clap clap clap clap clap cla
clap clap clap clap clap clap clap clap clap clap clap clap clap clap clap clap clap clap clap clap clap
clap clap clap clap clap clap clap clap clap clap clap clap clap clap clap clap clap clap clap clap clap
clap clap clap clap clap clap clap clap clap clap clap clap clap clap clap clap clap clap clap clap cla
clap clap clap clap clap clap clap clap clap clap clap clap clap clap clap clap clap clap clap clap clap c
clap clap clap clap clap clap clap clap clap clap clap clap clap clap clap clap clap clap clap clap cla
clap clap clap clap clap clap clap clap clap clap clap clap clap clap clap clap clap clap clap clap cl
clap clap woo-hoo!! clap clap clap clap clap clap clap clap clap clap clap clap clap clap cl
clap clap clap clap clap clap clap clap clap clap clap clap clap clap clap clap clap clap clap clap cla
clap clap clap clap clap clap clap clap clap clap clap clap clap clap clap clap clap clap clap clap clap
clap clap clap clap clap clap clap clap clap clap clap clap clap clap clap clap clap clap clap clap clap
clap clap clap clap clap clap clap clap clap clap clap clap clap clap clap clap clap clap clap clap cla
clap clap clap clap clap clap clap clap clap clap clap clap clap clap clap clap clap clap clap clap clap c
clap clap clap clap clap clap clap clap clap clap clap clap clap clap clap clap clap clap clap clap cla
clap clap clap clap clap clap clap clap clap clap clap clap clap clap clap clap clap clap clap clap cl
clap clap clap clap clap clap clap clap clap clap clap yeah!!clap clap clap clap clap clap clap cl
clap clap clap clap clap clap clap clap clap clap clap clap clap clap clap clap clap clap clap clap cla
clap clap clap clap clap clap clap clap clap clap clap clap clap clap clap clap clap clap clap clap clap
clap clap clap clap clap clap clap clap clap clap clap clap clap clap clap clap clap clap clap clap clap
clap clap clap clap clap clap clap clap clap clap clap clap clap clap clap clap clap clap clap clap cla
clap clap clap clap clap clap clap clap clap clap clap clap clap clap clap clap clap clap clap clap clap c
clap clap clap clap clap clap clap clap clap clap clap clap clap clap clap clap clap clap clap clap cla
clap clap clap clap clap clap clap clap clap clap clap clap clap clap clap clap clap clap clap clap cl
clap clap clap clap clap clap clap clap clap clap clap clap clap clap clap clap clap clap clap clap cla
clap clap clap clap clap clap clap clap clap clap clap clap clap clap clap clap clap clap clap clap clap
clap clap clap clap clap clap clap clap clap clap clap clap clap clap clap clap clap clap clap clap clap
clap clap clap clap clap clap clap clap clap clap clap clap clap clap clap clap clap clap clap clap cl
clap clap clap clap clap clap clap clap clap clap clap clap clap clap clap clap clap clap clap clap clap c
clap clap clap clap clap clap clap clap clap clap clap clap clap clap clap clap clap clap clap clap cla
clap clap clap clap clap clap clap clap clap clap clap clap clap clap clap clap clap clap clap clap clap c
clap clap clap clap clap clap clap clap clap clap clap clap clap woo-hoo!! clap clap clap clap c
clap clap clap clap clap clap clap clap clap clap clap clap clap clap clap clap clap clap clap clap cla
clap clap clap clap clap clap clap clap clap clap clap clap clap clap clap clap clap clap clap clap clap
clap clap clap clap clap clap clap clap clap clap clap clap clap clap clap clap clap clap clap clap clap
clap clap clap yeah!! clap clap clap clap clap clap clap clap clap clap clap clap clap clap clap cla
clap clap clap clap clap clap clap clap clap clap clap clap clap clap clap clap clap clap clap clap clap c

Neil Gaiman is the critically acclaimed, award-winning, *New York Times* bestselling author of numerous novels, stories, graphic novels, children's books, and screenplays. Originally from England, Gaiman now lives in the United States. He fears the Fraud Police.

Chip Kidd is a graphic designer and writer in New York City. He tries to make good art, but mostly just makes mistakes. Whether or not any of them are interesting, amazing, glorious, or fantastic is anyone's guess.